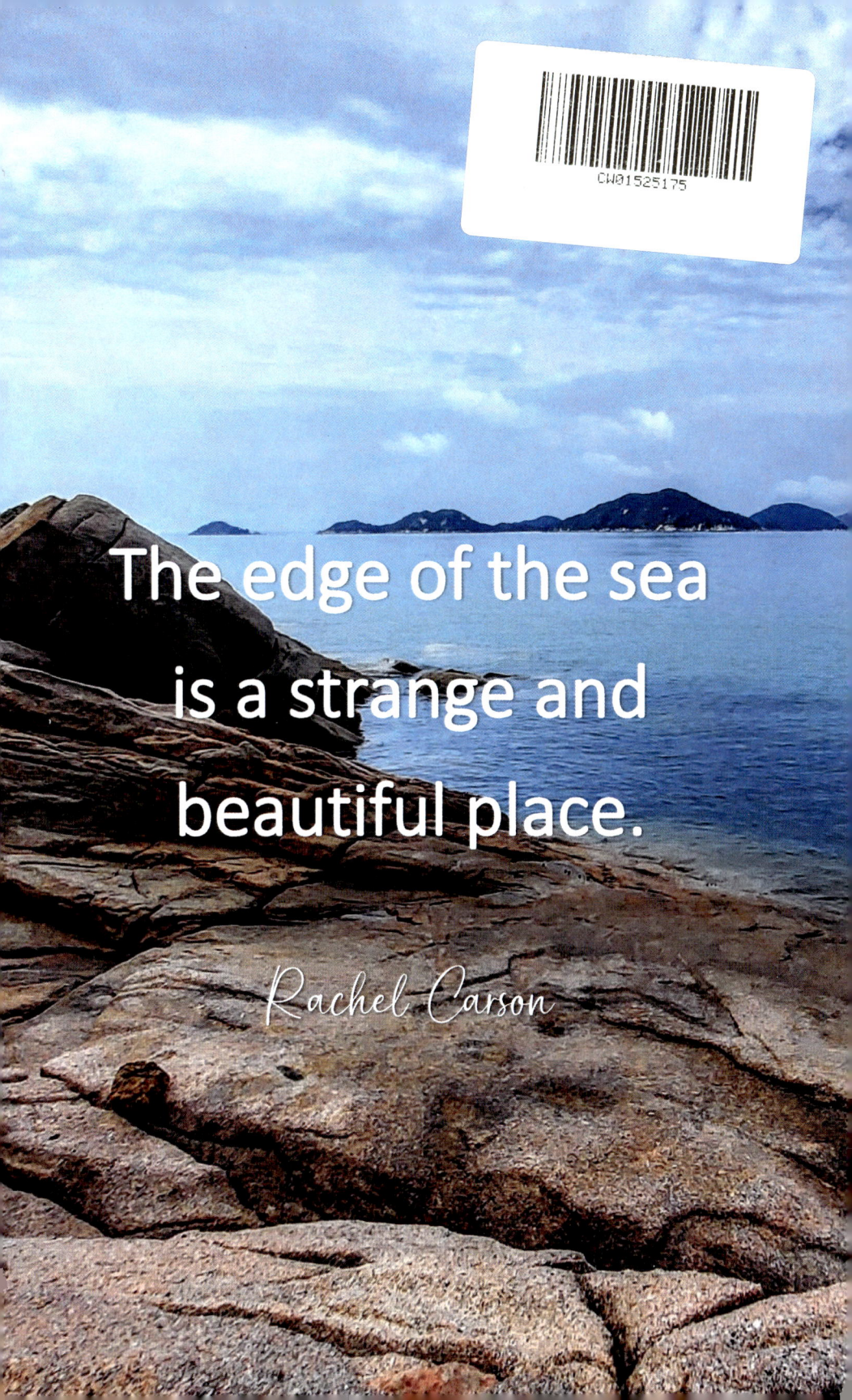

Copyright © 2022 Charmian Woodhouse.

First edition 2022.

Photos copyright © 2022 by Charmian Woodhouse and Cathy Cole.

Text copyright © 2022 Charmian Woodhouse.

Illustrations copyright © 2022 Charmian Woodhouse.

All rights reserved. This book or any portion thereof may not be reproduced or used in any manner whatsoever without the express written permission of the author except for the use of brief quotations in a book review.

For my amazing family;
and Cathy - thanks for all the adventures
and the excellent conversations along the way

# LANTAU COAST

## A coasteering journey around Lantau Island

*Charmian Woodhouse*

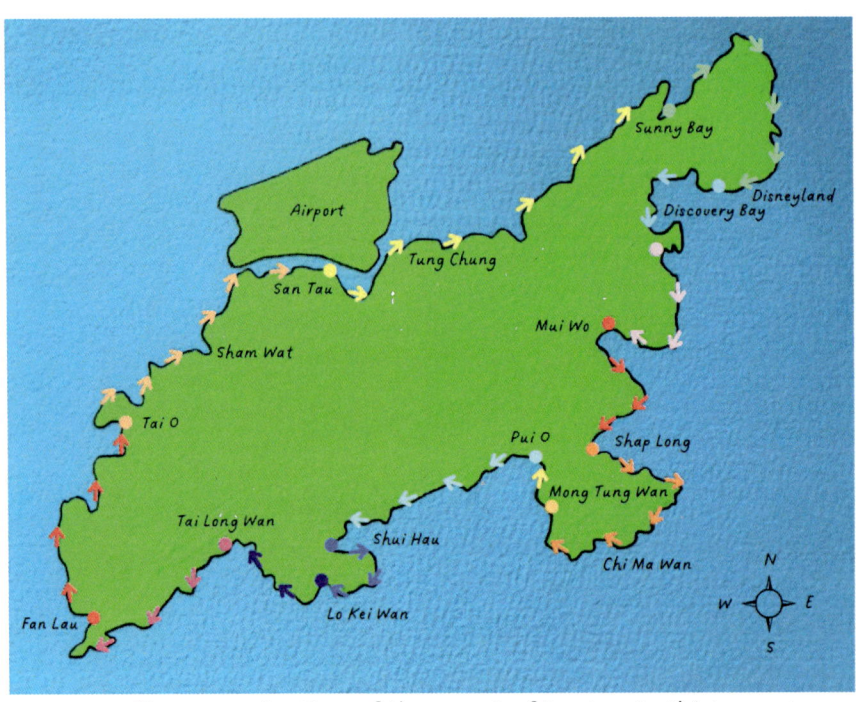

Circumnavigation of the coast of Lantau in thirteen stages

# LANTAU COAST

In the jade green waters of the South China Sea, at the mouth of the Pearl River, lies a beautiful island, Lantau. A mountainous island of rocky coastlines, beaches, mangroves, wetlands and rivers.

Lantau is the largest island of the Hong Kong archipelago; a sprawling collection of more than 250 islands scattered around the Kowloon peninsula. The islands carve the calm waters around Hong Kong into intricate shapes with curving bays and kilometres of rocky coastline.

Lantau is called the green jewel of Hong Kong. I have spent years exploring Lantau, running on the trails that criss-cross over the mountain peaks, rolling hills and lush valleys. Adding to the natural beauty of Lantau is the astounding variety of wildlife thriving on the island.

Cathy approached me with the idea of doing a coastal challenge together. She suggested that we do a version of a trail run I had done previously but to attempt to find a route closer to the coast. After exploring some rarely used, overgrown and impassable trails, we decided to travel directly on the water's edge, following the shoreline around the island.

The coastline of an island is a connection between land and sea. The intertidal zone is the bridge between the two, the meeting place of the aquatic world with terra firma. Lantau has scenic beaches and excellent coastal trails that many people enjoy. Others also frequent the coast to harvest food from the sea. But the coastline quickly becomes wild and remote as you move away from the beaches and trails and along the shoreline.

Coasteering is the sport of exploring a rocky coastline by climbing, scrambling, swimming and wading without the aid of a board or boat. It's a demanding and challenging activity.

It turned out to be a journey of discovery as we coasteered around Lantau, exploring the shoreline and documenting what we found along the way. We were amazed at the distinctive rocks, the beauty of nature and the interesting stories of this coastline.

We eventually circumnavigated Lantau in thirteen stages. We were challenged at times, enduring long hours of fatigue, traveling over difficult terrain and spending hours in icy water. There were also times of floating in calm currents with the sun warming our backs and the green mountains rising from the sea into a clear blue sky.

# THE PLAN

Colourful butterflies glide through the lush trees surrounding Cathy's garden. We sit outside, sipping fruit iced tea at a table laden with maps. There's a lot to think about before setting off on the first stage of our coasteer journey. It's time to study the tidal currents, wind, tides and weather patterns.

Scrutinizing satellite maps of the coastline, we divide the island's perimeter into distinct stages. Each stage will have its own challenges. Some will involve distances we are not sure we can cover in one day. Boulders line the coast in other areas, it's impossible to see from the maps if they will be too steep to climb. Cathy and I are already experienced open water swimmers and so our plan is to move along the coast when it's possible and to swim when the terrain gets too difficult to traverse.

Having an accurate understanding of the ocean currents is going to be vital to our plan. Swimming against a strong flow would slow us down or even make it impossible to continue. Some sections of the coast are inaccessible by land, and we could find ourselves stranded in a remote area by an opposing current. The tidal stream prediction maps are excellent, they give detailed information on the direction of the ocean currents at specific times of the day.

The first stage will take us from Mui Wo to Shap Long, a distance of about eight kilometres. We'll test out our gear, learn the basics and prepare for the next stages which will be much more challenging.

We know that we will need to enter and exit the water easily. Since the rocks along Lantau are covered with razor sharp oyster shells, we'll need to keep our shoes on, even while swimming. The shells can easily cause deep cuts, so we'll use gloves too.

Our safety gear also includes bright orange open water swimming buoys to make us visible to boats. We'll strap our buoys onto our backs with elasticated cord to free up our hands for climbing when we are on the land. Lastly, we need to devise a way to keep some of our gear waterproof including food, phones and first aid kits.

It's March. The tropical lightning storms will start soon with summer coming and even though the sea water is still quite cold, we decide to start immediately while the weather is calmer.

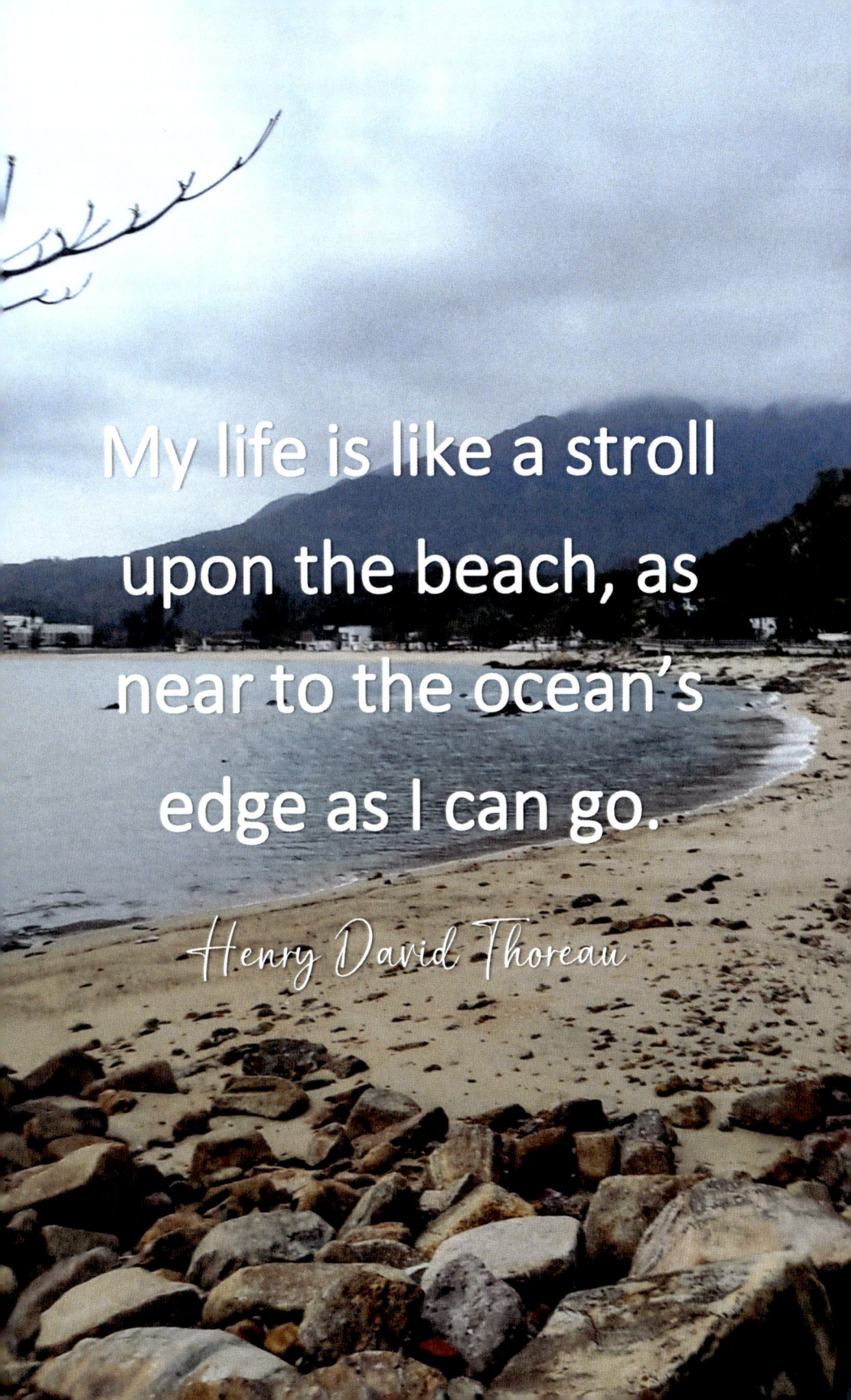

# THE BEGINNING

Mui Wo to Shap Long
7.7 km / 4.8 miles
4 hours

It's a cool, grey-sky day with a blustery monsoon wind blowing over the ocean. We meet at Mui Wo beach, feeling excited and nervous at what lies ahead. The treelined beach curves around the bay towards the village shops and ferry pier. In the distance, reddish-brown rocks line the coast on the far side of Silver Mine Bay.

As we near the start of the rocky coast, we come across a muntjac deer. The small, light brown deer glances at us, turns swiftly and bounds into the jungle. Muntjacs are a rare sighting as they are extremely shy animals. They have a distinctive barking call that echoes over the valleys. Seeing the deer feels like a good start to our journey.

Walking onto the rocks, we find out quickly that coasteering is like puzzle solving, each rock and boulder is a new challenge as we look for the best route forward. Sometimes we clamber up a rock only to find a steep drop on the other side, so we retreat to find another way.

At one place the rocks become too steep and I look down to find myself way too high up. Getting down again is heart stopping. It's time to get wet.

It feels strange to wade into the cool sea water as it floods our shoes. The drag of our backpacks and clothes pulls at us in the water. Kicking with shoes on is inefficient and so we concentrate on pulling strongly with our arms, trying to keep our feet relaxed and as streamlined as possible.

Monsoon winds make the water choppy on the coast

Climbing on the rocks towards Shap Long

A strong monsoon wind blows a blanket of clouds swiftly across the sky and makes the water choppy. We move steadily along the coast, scrambling, wading and swimming until we enter Shap Long Bay.

Windswept waves rush onto the coast, swirling around our legs as we navigate around the rocks, waist high in the water. We swim the last kilometre and walk out onto the beach with water squelching out of our shoes.

We've learned a lot and there are a few gear changes to make before starting the next stage, but we are euphoric. Travelling along the coast has given us a unique view of Lantau, we see the island in a new way. There is still a long way to go but we are on our way.

# LIFE ON THE COAST

The intertidal zone bustles with life. It's a place that responds to the daily changes of the tides as they rise and fall in harmony with the cosmic forces of the sun and moon.

Low tide brings a quiet hush to the coast as the rocks are exposed to the air. Barnacles close up tightly, waiting for the high tide to feed but this is a busy time for the many other creatures who feed on the nutrients left by the sea.

Chitons, marine molluscs, feed on the rocks. Some of them display homing behaviour, returning to the same home spot after roaming to eat. Their 'tongue' is called a radula and has rows of seventeen teeth which they use to scrape algae off the rocks.

At high tide the barnacles open to feed on micronutrients suspended in the water. They reach out with modified 'legs' to catch tiny particles of food, beating rhythmically as they draw the nutrients into their conical shells.

All along the coast, black kites, birds of prey, soar above the sea and dive down to pluck a fish from the water. White egrets and elegant herons stand still as stone along the shore, ever watchful for a silver fish to come within their reach. Sandpipers and delicate wagtails fly swiftly from rock to rock and occasionally there is a glimpse of iridescent blue as a kingfisher wings by.

Insects also populate the coast. Butterflies flit over the coastal waters. It's strange to see them so far from land. They also fly along the shore, obtaining salt from the moisture on the rocks.

Hundreds of sea slaters, also known as sea roaches, scuttle away from us as we approach, racing to hide in the cracks and crevices of the rocks. They are isopods and are closely related to woodlice. We briefly interrupt their microalgae feast as we pass by.

Sea slater

Chiton and barnacles

Red based Jezebel butterflies are common on the coast

# IN THE DEEP END

Chi Ma Wan Peninsula
Shap Long to Mong Tung Wan
8.0 km / 5.0 miles
10 hours

It's still dark when we board the inter-island ferry to Shap Long to start stage two. The ferry chugs sedately along the coast to dock at the pier just long enough for us to disembark. The sky lightens with dawn to reveal a cloudy day.

It's low tide and there's easy scrambling and wading all the way until we reach a tall pillar of rock at the point and turn west. Wind, rain and sea have carved out a honeycomb of hollows into the stone making a sculpture of the rock. It stands like a sentry on the coast, bravely facing the elements, a silent guardian of Lantau.

As we move forward, we can see the rocks and terrain changing. The boulders increase in size. They tower above our heads, and it soon becomes too difficult to navigate through them.

We enter the icy water. The inter-island currents have been pulling in colder water through the natural channel between the islands. As we swim, we study the coast to see if we can get out and continue on the rocks but the boulders are huge and so we keep swimming from bay to bay. I start to shiver and we climb out for a break. I can't stop shivering and we attempt to clamber through the rocks.

It's slow going weaving our way through the enormous boulders. Sometimes we need to wade through the water between the massive stones. I'm so cold, I don't want to get wet but there's no other way. We leap through waist high water from one submerged boulder to another, massive walls of rock surround us.

Weathered rock on Chi Ma Wan peninsula

Moving through icy water between huge boulders

We approach one boulder that is different from the boulders around us. It's an interesting rock, a mix of orange and pink stone. I clamber over it and then hear a heart-stopping yell as Cathy slips on the rock and I swing around to see that she has fallen onto the unforgiving rocks metres below and landed on her knee. I help her up and she sits on a boulder to recover. Her glasses are broken and there is a terrible white impact mark on her knee. I try to assess the situation as we might need to call for help.

A few minutes later an angry red bruise spreads down Cathy's leg. We realise that we will have to swim again, Cathy will not be able to continue along this extremely difficult terrain with an injured knee. It's a relief that she can still bend it, and nothing appears to be broken.

We carefully climb back into the water and start swimming. Luckily, I have warmed up a bit with the climbing that we did and the water feels slightly warmer as we move out of the channel and around the coast.

We pass a fisherman in his boat, and he calls out to us in Cantonese, trying to warn us about something but neither of us can understand. We find out soon though. Cathy yells out and tells me that she's been stung on her arm by a jellyfish. Her forearm turns bright red but is not too painful.

We swim across another bay, it takes us half an hour and we navigate around a rocky point. As the coast comes into view, we realise that there is yet another bay of swimming ahead of us.

Black kite

Massive stacked rocks on Chi Ma Wan peninsula

The beauty of the coast distracts us from our discomfort and fatigue. Birds of prey soar in the sky above us. We can hear birdsong from the shore and a bright butterfly flutters by.

Finally, we round the coast and head back inland. The rocks are easier to move over, and the cold water has appeared to help Cathy's knee, though it is still sore and slows her down.

We approach Sea Ranch, a failed luxury beach resort built in the seventies, now mostly deserted apart from a few residents. We slosh out onto the beach and walk across the sand.

It's not long before we need to enter the water again and we continue to swim along the coast. As we approach the abandoned village of Mong Tung Wan, the current pushes against us. It's impossible to move forward in the water and so we climb out and try the rocks again.

It's time to change our plans. We decide to hike out the last two kilometres along the coastal path. We've been on the coast for ten hours and with Cathy's injury, it's time to call it a day.

A dramatic pitch black basaltic dyke intrusion in granite rock on Chi Ma Wan peninsula

# LANTAU ROCKS

The Lantau Coast is a canvas showing the geological history of the island. If you were to travel from the white sands of Cheung Sha beach up to Lantau Peak and then over to Sunset Peak, you would travel over a geological history of over twenty-four million years.

Lantau has volcanic rock from four main ancient volcanic events including rock from a supervolcano to the east of Hong Kong. This supervolcano erupted 140 million years ago, one of only fifty known supervolcanoes in the world.

Most of the rock on Lantau was formed by a volcano which erupted even earlier, 146 - 148 million years ago. This volcano left a caldera, a cauldron shaped hollow, in the western and central part of Lantau.

The rocks of Lantau are a kaleidoscope of colours and patterns. Grey granite and speckled purplish-pink rhyolite line the coast and weathered sedimentary rock that looks like stone patchwork, blankets the coast on the west of the island. Iron seeps into cracks and fissures in the rock, outlining the joint planes in red and orange. White quartz veins make crystallised patterns on the ochre sandstone to form an artist's palette along the shore.

The coastline is incredibly varied with beaches, rocky shores, mudflats, seagrass beds and mangroves. Some areas have huge granite boulders heaped on top of each other and there are pebbly beaches. White sandy shores are patterned with black volcanic sand, sculptured by the wind and waves.

Jurassic stone near Tai O is the oldest rock on Lantau. Sedimentary rock formed by river sand and mud being laid down over eons, forming sandstone, siltstone and conglomerates - rocks made of mud and pebbles. Colourful layers of stone in red, orange, brown and black show the passage of time in this place.

The Lantau Dyke Swarm lies on the east side of the island. Fingers of rhyolite and basaltic andesite intrude between the granite rock of the island, forming parallel lines across the land. An ancient story told in stone of the history of Lantau.

> A beach is not only a sweep of sand, but shells of sea creatures, the sea glass, the seaweed, the incongruous objects washed up by the ocean.
>
> — *Henry Grunwald*

# OCEAN AND BEACH

Pui O to Shui Hau
7.0 km / 4.3 miles
4 hours

A brisk, icy wind blows down the slopes of Sunset Peak onto Pui O beach and out to sea. The tide is high and swimming will be the best option on this part of the coast.

Striking away from the beach, we are surrounded by the deep green sea reaching out to the horizon. The crisp, cool water is calming and we swim with the mountain on our right, rising into the clouds. We move steadily along the coast – shoals of silver fish flash by underneath.

Navigating our way through large boulders, avoiding hidden rocks underwater, we slow down as we approach Cheung Sha beach, enjoying the beauty of the boulders rising above the sea.

We walk up the sand to a beach cafe. Cathy enjoys a pot of Oolong tea and I sip a latte, wrapping my cold hands around the warming cup. Refreshed, we move on, strolling along the beach.

Breakers splash onto the sand in a froth of white bubbles. Minute sand-coloured crabs race along the wave line and schools of tiny fish frisk and dash through the shallows.

It's extremely relaxing to walk along the sand with a little easy scrambling as we go from beach to beach, passing Upper Cheung Sha, Lower Cheung Sha and Tong Fuk. There is only one difficult section where there is a sheer cliff, but we move up the rocks to find a way around and then slide down a steep slope back to the seaside.

A pebble beach appears, entirely covered with sea-smooth stones. There are speckled pebbles of red, orange, grey and charcoal black. Windswept waves break onto the pebbles in a rush and swirl. The water sucks out, rattling and knocking the stones in a wonderfully satisfying way, making rocky ocean music.

We stop for a while, silent and present in the moment, listening to the stones and watching the windswept bay. To the west, the Shui Hau bay is full to bursting with the colourful kites of the kite surfers making the most of the wind.

Waves move the pebbles to make beautiful rocky music as they knock against each other

Rocky beach near Tong Fuk

We survey the coast towards Shui Hau beach, it doesn't look too far away but when we round a corner, another large bay appears in front of us. This is part of the surprise and challenge of coasteering, what looks like just a little indent on the map can mean another hour of difficult scrambling along the shoreline.

A small, red brick temple with an emerald-green and pink roof, looks out over a tiny beach to the blue-grey waters of the bay. On the roof, golden dragons chase a flaming red pearl, symbol of wisdom, and red lanterns hang on either side of the open doorway.

The sun has come out and it's hot now at midday, so we enter the cooling water and swim across the bay to the opposite beach. Small rolling waves churn up onto the shore, thick with lime-green seaweed and we saunter along the beach to Shui Hau.

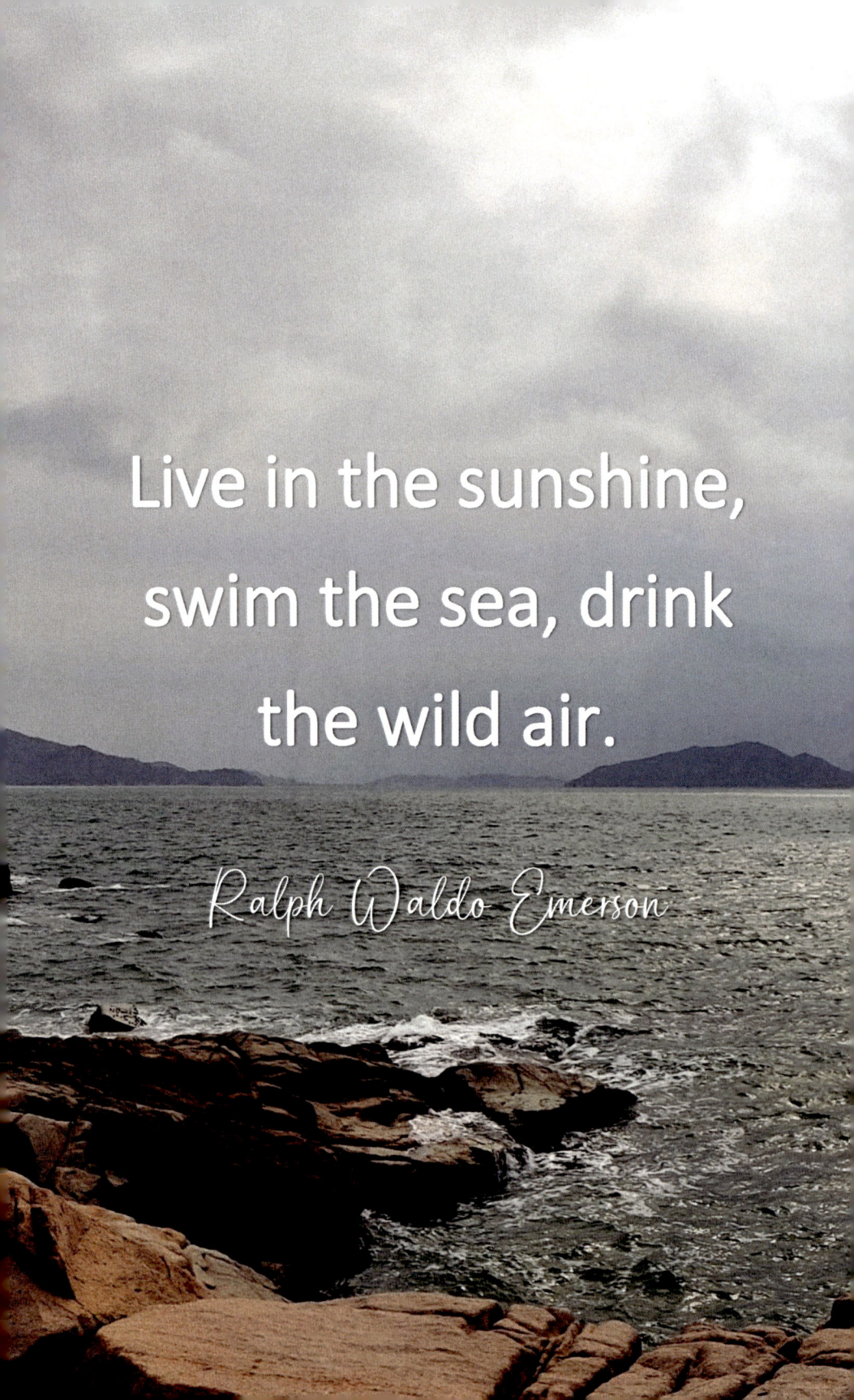

# WIND AND WAVES

Shui Hau Peninsula
Shui Hau to Lo Kei Wan 4.4 km / 2.7 miles
Tung Wan to Tai Long Wan 2.6 km / 1.6 miles
6 hours

We start early, at sunrise, to make the most of the low tide. We feel so connected to the ebb and flow of the tides on our journey as they constantly change the conditions on the coast.

The ocean currents move rivers of water past the land, changing direction with the tides. It's all intricately intertwined and dynamic and happens every moment of every day.

The tidal flats at Shui Hau lie exposed now but the tide has turned, and the water is slowly but steadily returning. The shore is full of life. Baby-blue soldier crabs feed in the puddles. If threatened, they scrabble in the muddy sand with their pale orange spindly legs and twirl in a dancers' circular motion to disappear into the sand.

It's not long before we round the eastern side of the peninsula and need to enter the water with the incoming tide making it too difficult to move over the larger boulders edging the land. There is a fresh sea wind, the water is choppy and cool and there is an expansive bay ahead of us to swim across. We aim for the remote point.

Soldier crab

As we approach the rocks to climb out, Cathy realises that she doesn't have her gloves on. The rocks are covered with extremely sharp oyster shells and barnacles and gloves are a necessity, so she stops on a submerged rock to put them on.

A set of waves washes in around us. I grab Cathy's arm to try to stabilise her, but the powerful waves push us off the rock and towards the shore. I wash up over the rocks, trying to find a grip, to control my tumbling rush in the foaming water. I end up wedged up against a large boulder and brace against it to take the force of the waves against my back.

Waves come in sets, with several waves rolling in and then a lull before the next set. So I relax and wait for the set to finish, bracing for each wave that crashes against me, pushing me up against the boulder, waiting for the lull which will give me time to climb out safely.

Cathy is swept up over some rocks and bangs her injured knee. She's in pain but manages to gain her footing and I call out to her, telling her when the next wave is about to hit, to prepare for the swirl and splash of water around her.

The water quietens in the lull, and I scramble out of the water onto the rocks higher up. Cathy stands up and moves out too. We sit down on a boulder to recover. Blood seeps out of Cathy's bandaged knee. Her knee is still tender and sore from last week's fall, it must be extremely painful now.

Cathy exclaims in dismay that she has lost her phone. It has fallen out of her bag and is lost in the green-grey waters. We stop to rest, eating and drinking, taking time to recover, but now it's time to move forward again.

We clamber over the rocks for a while, but we are stopped by a steep, impassable cliff. In the shallows I can see a large jellyfish floating just offshore so we move to the left to avoid it and enter the water carefully. It's going to be another long swim.

Where there is one jellyfish, there are sure to be more. I turn my head to breathe and find myself covered with fine white hairs, a fringe of net covering my face. I realise that I have entangled myself in the long tentacles of a ghost jellyfish. Panicked, I brush them away and I can feel my lips start to tingle and become numb. I start to laugh, my go-to response in dealing with challenging circumstances. I feel another sting on my calf. The stings aren't too bad, I can't feel my lips but it's not really a problem. Over the course of the afternoon, the numb sensation subsides and goes away.

On the other side of the bay, we can see that the rocks are still too steep and so we continue in the water. At each rocky point between the bays, the current suddenly changes direction and starts to flow against us with the movement of the sea interacting with the unyielding curves of the coastline. At times, we are almost stationary with little progress as we fight against the push of the water around us. Whenever that happens, we change direction and move closer to the rocks where the current seems to lessen, and we can move forward into the next bay.

As we near Lo Kei Wan we can feel the tidal current has changed and is now continuously flowing against us. We leap from rock to rock, grabbing onto boulders and pushing against them to propel ourselves forward in the water.

Arriving at Lo Kei Wan beach, there are campers relaxing on the sand and people swimming in the waves. We have spent five hours travelling four kilometres and are exhausted, so we decide to continue on the coastal trail with panoramic sea views. We will come back another day to coasteer on the last section of the Shui Hau peninsula.

Lo Kei Wan beach is the site where a people-smuggling freighter called the Sen On, full of Vietnamese people, was beached in 1979. The captain and crew had abandoned the ship near Macau to avoid the Hong Kong Marine Police. Those left on board had to navigate to Hong Kong with no knowledge of how to operate the vessel. They aimed for the beach and drove the freighter onto the sand. Thankfully, the vessel didn't capsize and everyone made it off safely. Seeing the beach now, pristine and with beachgoers enjoying the sand and surf, it's hard to imagine what it must have been like on that day.

We enter the coast again at Tung Wan with the prison rising in an imposing mass of concrete and high security fences in front of us. We wade across a shallow bay, walk across the pier and along the stone wall and then the siren starts. We look at each other, feeling strangely guilty, as the piercing sound of the siren wails on and on.

Entering the water

Sea mango flower

Beach naupaka flower

Veins of quartz crystals

Continuing across the prison beach and then back on the rocky shore, the tide is going out now. The constant rush of water has receded and a peaceful calm descends on the coast. We stroll along a wave cut ledge with a cliff towering above us, its sheer sides creating a natural wall along the water's edge.

A variety of plants flourish on the coast, all beautifully adapted to the seaside. These plants are salt and flood resistant and can handle windy conditions. Pioneer plants like beach naupaka grace the coast with their delicate white fan flowers. Its fruit falls in the water to travel on the ocean currents to propagate on other shores.

The lovely coral centred, white flowers of the deadly poisonous sea mango cluster in bouquets between the dark green leaves of the coastal tree. It has bright red fruit which is extremely toxic and deadly if eaten.

The rock changes from grey boulders to brick red, orange and sulphur yellow stone. Veins of quartz appear out of the rock like crystalised skeletons making intricate patterns through the stone.

As we near the village, we pass some people harvesting gooseneck barnacles, prising them off in chunks with screwdrivers. They are also called Buddha's Hands because they look like two hands held together in prayer. They are cooked into a soup and are considered a delicacy and are a valuable resource, though one lady we talk to says she doesn't like to eat them herself.

And so we finish our day on the coast, walking up the beach to the sleepy seaside village of Tai Long Wan.

Gooseneck barnacles

Red oxidized iron makes flame patterns on the rock near Tai Long Wan

> In every out-thrust headland, in every curving beach, in every grain of sand there is the story of the earth.
>
> *Rachel Carson*

# CURRENTS

Tai Long Wan to Fan Lau
7.0 km / 4.3 miles
8 hours

We arrive at Tai Long Wan beach as the rising sun saturates the sky with a rosy peach glow. Clear green water reflects all the colours of the vivid early morning light. The tide is out and there is a quiet hush on the coast.

Entering the water, we swim across one bay and then another. The current is strong and is moving in the direction that we want to go in. We relax in the flow and watch the coastline passing by.

Sitting on a huge boulder to have a snack and rest, we explore the rocks, taking photos of the interesting formations and different colours of the stone. Back in the water again, my heart sinks as I realise that I haven't packed my phone into my waterproof buoy before entering the water and I pull it out of my pocket, it's soaking wet and dead. All I can do is ruefully laugh about it.

A fisherman in a boat sees us in the deep water and motors up to check on us. We smile, touched by his concern and tell him we are going to Tai O.

Climbing through the rocks on a stony beach, Cathy lands badly on her foot and rolls her ankle on the loose pebbles. She gasps in pain and sits down to recover. We enter the water again, the cool water once again helping with the inflammation and pain. Swimming up onto the next beach, Cathy tapes her ankle and I help to bandage it for extra support.

We know that the currents will be changing and turning against us in two hours and so we press on, racing against the tide. There is another promontory to navigate around before we arrive at Fan Lau. We make it in good time, splashing out onto the beach, walking past the ghost crab burrows and the purple beach morning glory flowers.

Ocean currents with speed in knots

| | |
|---|---|
| ← | 0-0.5 |
| ← | 0.5-1.0 |
| ← | 1.0-1.5 |
| ← | 1.5-2.0 |
| ← | 2.0-2.5 |
| ← | 2.5 + |

Volcanic tuff near Tai Long Wan with Lantau Peak in the distance

Ghost crab

Beach morning glory

Each single layer of earth tells a story that's all its own. The sands of the ancient beaches have changed into strata of stone.

*Hugh Auchineloss Brown*

# BEAUTIFUL ROCK

Tai O to Tung Chung
11.8 km / 7.3 miles
9 hours

Stilt houses line the bay of Tai O, perched above the mudflats and tidal waters. Mangrove trees grow all around the village, their aerial roots rising out of the dark mud.

Tai O is a fishing village with a long and colourful history. It is nestled in a valley surrounded by gentle sloping mountains. You can still see the remains of the salt pans where salt was produced. There was a bustling salt smuggling trade during the eighteenth century.

The Tai O river splits to form a small island and then flows into an expansive bay where rare pink dolphins can be found. Indo-Pacific humpback dolphins are white but the blood flow in vessels near their skin gives them the appearance of being bubblegum pink. The waters around Tai O are quiet today though.

The sandstone and siltstone of the Tai O Formation are the oldest rocks on Lantau. With vibrant colours of orange, red and black, it makes exquisite earth art. We are relieved that it is easy to walk along this part of the coast because there is a lot of rubbish floating in the water and neither of us want to get in.

Piercing cicada song fills the air and occasionally a large black and yellow spotted cicada flies past us to settle on an overhanging tree. Animals and insects that make their home on land mix with the strange and wonderful sea creatures living in the intertidal zone.

Crabs, mussels and oysters intermingle with insects and birds. Egrets fish, black kites soar above, their descending, whistling trill sounding out over the chatter of sandpipers, piping their sweet song and lifting swiftly to swoop and dive away over the water as we approach.

Sand piper

As we move along the coast, the rocks become even more interesting. Flames set in stone, blaze on crystal tuff rock. Red and white quartz and ochre boulders, covered with honeycomb shapes, are vivid against a grey sky and calm sea and framed by the long line of the Hong Kong–Zhuhai–Macau Bridge stretching into the distance.

We come across a 'pirates' raft that someone has made, creatively using the flotsam and jetsam littering the coast, complete with a figurehead constructed out of the head and bust of a mannequin.

We walk past large chunks of rotting meat and wonder why it has been thrown into the ocean to land up on these shores. Later Cathy finds out that it's the work of smugglers who throw their cargo overboard if there is a risk of being caught on their clandestine trips. This coast has a long history of smugglers.

Black spotted cicada

Little egret

Large bamboo frames add to the difficulty of climbing over the rocks. We clamber over them, avoiding sharp edges. Boating rubbish, life jackets and life rings are wedged into the rocks all along this stretch of coast.

And so it is a refreshing change to see the water eventually becoming cleaner and the rubbish diminishing. The densely wooded mountains plunge into the sea, deep green trees cover every part of the steep slopes.

We walk over rock that is so unusual that we stop in our tracks, amazed. A stone quilt blankets the coast, made of pale pink sandstone squares surrounded by reddish-orange limonite ruffles. It's a geological wonder.

Our first stop is Sham Wat. We can see a few rocky points ahead of us and try to guess which one will be the entrance to the bay that curves into the village, but with each point we reach, we can see the coast ribboning ahead of us. Finally, we round the point into Sham Wat bay, passing a fisherman who calls out to us from his boat, asking where we have been and where we are going and giving us a big thumbs up and smile as he passes by.

We wade into the shallow bay, the sea floor is completely covered with thick, black mud. If we stop, we immediately start sinking into the ooze and it's incredibly difficult to pull our feet out as the mud clings with surprising strength and nearly pulls our shoes off. Each step is a struggle and so we move closer to the trees growing in the shallows. The mud is a little more stable here and we manage to move towards the rocks and then climb over a wall and find the path that leads into the village.

Bamboo frame on the coast

Weathered rock near Sham Wat

Red Limonite outlines pink coarse-grained sandstone to create a stone quilt on the coast near Sham Wat

Rock made red by oxidised iron

Honeycomb weathered rock

Rock flames on crystal tuff with weathering joints

We have been planning to enjoy tofu fa at Sham Wat for weeks, a cold tofu dessert, topped with orange sugar. We thought we might miss our treat by arriving too early in the day, estimating that it would take us two hours to get here from Tai O. But it has taken us double as long and so everything is open and ready for business by the time we wash up.

It's so wonderful to sit down on bright pink plastic chairs and to enjoy a bowl of tofu fa with a cold drink. It feels strange to be back among people after travelling over such a remote and solitary coast.

Paying our bill and walking straight back onto the coast, we pass a sign that warns about the dangerous sinking mud. We keep as close to the tree line as possible, once getting bogged down, but staying calm and moving slowly to escape the mud. The coast soon changes back to rocky shores and we are on our way again.

I can feel something in my shoe, perhaps a rock or shell and stop to take it off and am horrified to see a tiny silver fish, terribly squashed. It probably swam into my shoe as I was trudging through the mud.

Tofu fa dessert at Sham Wat

Holly mangrove

Along the rocks we come across wreckage from a boat and we can see a shipwreck submerged murkily in the water. Sharp corroded metal lurks ominously in the shallows. There's a gap in the rocks here, too big to jump over. The sea rushes in turbulently between the steep stone walls.

A few weathered planks of wood have been laid over the gap, they tilt and wobble as we place our weight on them. It's too dangerous to try to swim here with all that sharp metal from the submerged wreck, so we decide to risk the makeshift wooden bridge.

After a few heart-stopping moments we make it over safely, deciding to stay low, sitting on the bridge and shifting over it. Risking a few splinters is better than falling into the chasm.

Among the rocks, the holly mangrove flowers unfurl from the base, the maturing spire of buds turn from shades of magenta to lime green, ivory and then finally a bright indigo.

Now the land changes and we have some steep, difficult water entries, snagging our pants on the sharp oysters, tearing them. We can't see the sea floor, the water is too murky. We find out by trial whether we will find rock underneath our next step or end up swimming in deep water. We develop the 'crab swim', moving forward in a crouching sideways wade, feeling for submerged rocks with our feet. This keeps our knees out of harm's way of the hidden rocks underwater.

The Hong Kong–Zhuhai–Macau Bridge looms above us. Immense concrete pillars rise out of the water and the curving line of the road veers away into the distance. There is a brilliant flash of blue as a white-throated kingfisher flies up into the trees.

The village of Sha Lo Wan is guarded by a tall dragon constructed out of recycled wood and plastic bottles. It's a work of art standing tall against the blue sky and surrounded by colourful fishing boats lying high and dry on the sand. Behind it, the Pa Kong Ancient Temple flags wave in the sun and wind, bright yellow, pink and blue.

It's low tide again and we can see thousands of snails in their pointed shells feeding on the sand and tiny crabs scuttle into their holes as we pass. A jellyfish is stranded on the beach with exquisite geometric patterns, shining silver among the green seaweed and muddy shells. Airplanes roar into the sky as we near the airport.

Peace comes with the ebb of the tide, calmness, stillness pervades. The boulders give way to pebbles and the skyscrapers of Tung Chung come into view. People are out, enjoying the fresh air and children are playing and exploring, discovering the fascinating sea creatures that live here. We walk onto the path leading into town to find our friend Annie and her son, Landon, here to meet us. They hand out oranges, the sweet citrus fruit tastes magical on our tongues.

Sha Lo Wan Dragon

Hong Kong-Zhuhai-Macau Bridge

# SKYSCRAPERS

Tung Chung to Sunny Bay
17.8 km / 11.0 miles
8 hours

Blue sky and calm, it's going to be a scorching hot day. This stage will have challenges that we haven't had to deal with yet. We will be passing Tung Chung, a bustling town with towering skyscrapers. We are not sure if the building and land reclamation sites will push us away from the coast.

We hike back to San Tau. It's low tide and the mud flats are exposed, revealing the tracks of the pointed snails and scuttling crabs. Gorgeous fat sea hares, a type of sea slug, feast on the algae in the mud, their faces squelched firmly in the fertile ooze.

Sea hare

Tung Chung skyscrapers line the coast

We pick our way carefully through the rocks, sinking into the mud, walking along bright green seaweed carpets. Mangrove tree seedlings have taken root, tiny green leaves grow from the pointed propagules.

It's surreal to be wading through murky green water with the backdrop of the mountains and thousands of windows towering over us from the skyscrapers that form a wall of concrete and glass behind us.

Tung Chung used to be a small fishing village, remote and isolated. Now the town is home to tens of thousands of people. A myriad of apartments rise one above another in huge skyscrapers. Tung Chung means 'Eastern Stream'. The stream is still full of river life and flows quietly into the bay.

Tung Chung fort, complete with rusting cannons, once guarded the bay from smugglers and was also there to stop the opium trade along the coast. During the Qing Dynasty it was used by pirates, becoming their base until the surrender of Cheung Po Tsai. He had been abducted by pirates as a teenager but rose through their ranks to command a large fleet of pirate vessels. Eventually he surrendered, became a naval colonel, and helped the government to combat pirates for the rest of his life.

The impressive construction of the airport dominates the view now. It was built on reclaimed land right next to the town, assimilating the islands of Chek Lap Kok and Lam Chau. The most expensive airport to ever be constructed, millions of cubic metres were dredged during construction. This was done in just two and a half years.

And so it was surprising to find ourselves walking into the past, finding the historic fishing village of Ma Wan Chung nestled on the coast, an oasis of history and tradition surrounded by the intense development of the still growing town.

Ma Wan Chung Village

Walking through the closely built village houses, along winding narrow paths and past potted gardens, village life continues uninterrupted here. In the little bay next to the village, the Saturday morning swimmers splash in the sea next to the pier. Some wade in the shallows, others strike out into deeper water. We join them and continue on our way.

Joggers run along the Tung Chung seafront, groups of people go through their exercises together and people walk past with their coffee cups. Searing heat radiates from the ground, and we can see a huge construction area ahead of us, surrounded by a tall, corrugated iron fence. We peer over and can see the water, but we can't get near it.

Walking past a coffee shop, we stop to get an ice coffee, feeling out of place standing in the queue in our coasteer gear with our swimming buoys strapped to our backs. The icy cold drink is refreshing as we trek along the straight cement path. Trains rush past periodically in a roar of noise and wind. The sky is clear blue, the sun burns down on our heads.

Finally, we find ourselves next to the green sea again. The massive Hong Kong–Zhuhai–Macau Bridge towers sinuously above our heads. We find some informal steps leading down a very steep hill. Three metal ladders have been ingeniously tied to the hillside leading to a small private beach. There are some people here, enjoying the water and relaxing in tents. We splash straight back into the refreshing water and bob across the bay, passing fishermen, swimming wide to avoid their lines reaching into the depths.

The tide is waning and the tombolo will soon be exposed to become a land-bridge to Cheung Sok Island

We find our way around the desalination plant and begin the last peninsula for the day. It's high tide and we find that the current has strengthened and it sweeps us along the coast. All we have to do is float in the watery conveyor belt.

A remote beach appears ahead of us and we are surprised to see some people relaxing on the sand who welcome us with huge smiles and waves. We trudge up onto the sand and are invited to join them, they offer us cold drinks. We crack open a can and have a chat. After lots of laughter and group photos, we wave goodbye and walk back into the water.

The current is even stronger now, it's a free ride all the way up the coast. As we near the promontory, the current hits into the land and breaks into two, pushing out in opposite directions and we can feel it turning back on us, so we clamber out and stop to enjoy the view from the rocks.

We are on Cheung Sok, a small island which is connected to Lantau by a tombolo, a shallow sand bank which gets exposed at low tide. As we round the corner, we see a group of people on the other side, waiting for low tide to walk across. We stop and look at each other and wave.

Splashing over the tombolo to finish our day on the coast, we can see huge tree trunks sticking vertically out of the water of the shallow bay, remnants from a lumber factory long ago.

Timber storage poles in Sunny Bay

# UNDER THE BRIDGE

Sunny Bay to Disneyland
10.0 km / 6.2 miles
7 hours

An early bus to Tung Chung and then a train to Sunny Bay sees us arrive on the coast ready for a new day. We are both extremely excited about the route ahead and nervous too. I have spent ages studying the strength and direction of the currents as they change throughout the day in response to the tides.

A narrow channel surrounded by larger bodies of water on either side of the island creates perfect conditions for extremely strong tidal currents under the bridge that connects Lantau to the New Territories.

Swimming towards Tsing Ma Bridge

Tsing Ma Bridge

An opposing current coming up the coast from the south-west also affects the conditions of the sea here. We can swim at about 1.5 knots and the currents here can get to 3 knots or more. It would be impossible to swim against such a strong current flowing against us.

At Sunny Bay, fishermen are already standing on the rocks with their lines out. It's high tide, so we enter the water straight away. The water is calm here, no jellyfish are in sight and there's a lovely current helping us on our way.

Out in the channel huge tankers sail past. We round the point and the impressive geometric view of the Tsing Ma Bridge appears. The criss-crossing of cables in perfect tension dominates the skyline.

We climb out onto a beach and Cathy's phone buzzes. Her colleague who lives across the channel can see us through his binoculars from his apartment. We send a big wave in his direction.

Swimming up to the bridge, we are suddenly met by an exceptionally strong push of water. We can see a ramp not far away and we have to swim with all our strength to make headway against the flow. My heart is racing by the time I can get my toe on the ground, but we still have to fight to move forward up the ramp. Catching our breath, we sit down on a boulder. The view is amazing.

Clear green-blue water sweeps under the bridge and we can see the dancing water showing where there is a meeting of two opposing currents, one being swept close to shore and one racing out towards Hong Kong Island in a turbulent rush.

As we continue along the shore, we come across massive parallel fingers of rock reaching out into the sea. We climb up and over each one. Sometimes they are too steep to climb down so we leap into the sea to swim to the next climbable part.

The sea is like a washing machine, a strong wind whips up the water around us. We dodge around jellyfish and each section we swim is tiring and challenging. We bounce and bob our way down the coast with incessant wavelets splashing into our faces.

Across the sea we can see the city skyscrapers shining in the sun on Hong Kong Island. Finally, we have an easy walk to Disneyland along the seawall. As we climb over the railing onto the pier, we are surrounded by Disney music on our way down the paved avenue to the station.

Looking out to Hong Kong Island

Using fishermen's ropes to navigate a steep cliff

# DISNEYLAND TO DISCOVERY BAY

Disneyland to Discovery Bay
7.5 km / 4.7 miles
7 hours

It's raining, heavy drops of rain splash onto the ground. Walking through the damp Saturday morning crowds on our way to Disneyland, we see another person on his way to the coast, a fisherman with his rods and wheeled cooler heading to the peace and quiet of the coast.

We start with a river crossing. We can see jellyfish in the water and dark patches of red tide, showing where myriad microorganisms are floating in the bay. When the conditions are right, the unicellular microorganisms multiply and swamp large areas of the coast, staining the water to a shade of reddish brown. Some red tides glow when agitated and at night, shimmering flowing lines of bright blue bio-luminescence shine in the wakes of the ferries. Most red tides are not harmful, but we don't feel like putting our faces into the water. At times it's so thick the water looks black.

Passing Disneyland

Silver sky and calm sea

The calm, treacle smooth water feels cool and there's a stillness in the air. The rain has passed by, silver clouds cover the sky. The conditions are totally different from last week. Everything is serene and tranquil as we swim, walk and climb over rocks on our way along the coast.

We see more jellyfish and try to avoid them, but unfortunately Cathy gets stung on her neck, a red rash quickly appears. The hills above us look deserted, there is very little human impact here. All we can hear are the birds singing.

We arrive at Discovery Bay, the resort town towers above us. The dragon boat teams splash their paddles simultaneously as they race across the bay in long, narrow boats. The voice of their leader, shouting out commands, carries over the water. Sailing boats cruise slowly through the windless bay. Happy children play on the beach, families picnic on the sand, the boat club is busy.

As we swim past a pier, a white-throated kingfisher swoops down and lands on a pillar in front of us. Its white throat is vivid against its chocolate brown feathers and brilliant blue back, the brightest azure turquoise. It stays for a while, watching us.

White-throated kingfisher

Discovery Bay

We can see evidence of erosion on the coast, cliffs are washed out, tree roots exposed. A ferry passes and soon after, fierce waves from the boat's wake crash onto the land. The water is clear and green again, there is no red tide here and there are some quiet beaches with views of the open sea and islands.

We swim around the marina and arrive at the steps. We're freezing after our long swim and there's a long wait for the next ferry home, so we walk back into town to get a hot drink to warm up before boarding the little ferry which chugs its way along the coast, taking us home.

For the next three stages we will be returning to parts of the coast to complete some sections that we have not coasteered on yet because of injuries or weather conditions. It's time to go back to explore these coastlines.

# BATS AND JELLYFISH

Chi Ma Wan Peninsula Part 2
Mong Tung Wan to Pui O
2.4 km / 1.5 miles
3 hours

Hiking on the coastal trail to Mong Tung Wan, we look out at the early morning sun glinting on the ocean and shining on the neighbouring islands in the distance.

The last time we were on the Chi Ma Wan peninsula, Cathy had injured her knee on the rocks and I had been battling the cold from being in the icy sea water for too long. After ten exhausting hours we had abandoned the coast and had hiked out along the coastal trail, leaving the last short section into Pui O for another day. So we feel that we are dealing with unfinished business today.

Swimming towards Pui O

Learning more about the geology of the island has been fascinating and we see the land with enlightened eyes. It makes the land feel alive to know that a fault line passes through the valley connecting Chi Ma Wan peninsula with the rest of Lantau.

We arrive at Mong Tung Wan, an abandoned village. It must have been a lovely place at one time. One house lies ghostly still, surrounded by the remains of a beautiful garden. There are polished stone tables outside and a water buffalo statue lies discarded among the greenery with views of the sea peeking through the trees. Inside, there are still cups and plates in the kitchen, a beautifully painted screen tilts against the wall, the birds and flowers fading in the gloom.

The abandoned houses here and there along the shores of Lantau lie quietly in disrepair. They are too isolated and remote to be homes to people who are now used to city conveniences. As their occupants age or move away, the homes lie empty with the jungle reclaiming them slowly over time.

Outside, the sky shines blue behind the cotton wool clouds. Dogs play on the sand and ladies sit together, chatting and laughing. We head off, moving away from the sound of Saturday conversations, and walk into the golden morning ahead of us.

We weave our way through the boulders on the sand and are hit by a terrible smell. A baby finless porpoise lies decomposing on the sand. Flies buzz, intestines spill out, blank eyes stare. It's such a sad sight, but we take photos so that we can report it to the nature conservation people.

Finless porpoises, otherwise known as 'sea pigs' are rare in Hong Kong with the population estimated to be around two hundred. They are grey, quite small and chubby, only growing to about two metres in length. They have a dorsal groove on their backs instead of a dorsal fin and they are very shy and elusive animals. Unfortunately, there has been an increase in strandings around Hong Kong in recent years.

Moving on, we clamber over gorgeous climbable boulders splashed by green-blue sea. There's a light breeze. We have time on our side and with only a short distance to cover, we're free to explore.

We climb rocks and jump back into the water, chat about books, art, geology, wherever the conversation flows. Long roots hang down rocky cliffs, exposed to the air. A sea cave comes into view and we can see a narrow beach rising up into the shadows.

We swim up to the opening, small waves rush in noisily, echoing in the cave. We enter, twisting through a tight squeeze in-between immovable rock walls. A chittering, squeaking sound and a strange pungent odour fills the air.

At the top of the stone wall, a black hole disappears into the rock wall and we can just see the flit of a bat swirling in the darkness. The roof of the cave is covered with bats, huddled up in the gloom. They jostle each other, occasionally one swirls in the air to land in the crowd, setting off a chorus of squeaks. Rousette fruit bats are megabats, also known as dog-faced bats or flying foxes and have sweet furry faces. They are the only megabats to use echolocation.

A rat scuttles on the floor of the cave, perhaps the reason that the bats are making so much noise. We look out, past the protective rock walls to the bright blue of the sky and sea. It's all so incredibly wild and beautiful.

On the rocky point, we can see the Pui O bay in front of us. We climb out onto a rock and sit quietly with a snack, enjoying the sun warming our backs and listening to the susurration of the water on the rocks.

A huge spotted dome of a flower jellyfish rolls up from the deep, next to our rock. It tips over, exposing its tentacle frill and submerges again. While we watch, we can see it appearing and sinking periodically. It appears to be able to rise and sink at will, something I've never thought about before. My preconceived idea was that jellyfish simply moved with the currents, mindlessly pulsing along.

Bat sea cave

A lion's mane jellyfish appears next, with seaweed caught in its tentacles. This one has a more potent sting and is one to watch out for. The jellyfish arrive in Hong Kong around this time each year, brought in by the clockwork of the oceanic timetable.

Cloud shadows move rapidly over the sea and the dark green slopes of the mountains rise up in front of us, covered with a topping of soft, meringue cloud peaks.

We swim to the coast and continue on the land. We can see another flower jellyfish in the water, in the shallows, right next to the rock. I splash into the water to get a closer look. The jellyfish is dead but something is hidden in the short fleshy tentacles. I reach over and touch it with my gloved hand and it tips over, turning upside down in the water.

There are brittle stars in the folds and creases of the tentacles. I reach in and scoop the jellyfish up gently, holding it so we can get a good look. After doing all we can to avoid jellyfish, it feels surreal to be so close to one. Brittle stars are echinoderms, related to starfish. They are kleptoparasites, stealing food from the jellyfish as they hitchhike around in their tentacles.

The tide is ebbing, we wade, chest deep, carefully feeling our way forward over rocks in the opaque water. This is my favourite way of moving on the coast, leaping like astronauts from rock to rock, almost buoyant in the chest high water.

Arriving at Pui O beach, we feel totally relaxed. As we walk past the information signboard, we are interested to see that it features a poster of all the dangerous sea creatures found in Hong Kong waters. Sea snakes, lethal stonefish, lionfish, waspfish, moray eels, bristle worms, the dangerous cone shell and the lion's mane jellyfish.

Hong Kong's temperate winters and tropical summers, along with the mixing of the Kuroshio, Taiwan and Hainan ocean currents create perfect conditions for an incredible diversity of sea life along its shores.

Flower jellyfish

Brittle stars

# CRYSTAL CLEAR WATER

Shui Hau Peninsula Part 2
Lo Kei Wan to Tung Wan
2.8 km / 1.7 miles
4 hours

It's a steep hike down to Lo Kei Wan beach where tents are lined up under the shady trees. It's early, the campers are still sleeping. The sun is rising, lighting the fleecy clouds.

We start by walking into the crystal clear water, weaving our way around the rocks in the sand. It's easy to get into a gentle current which moves us steadily along the coast. Huge heaped-up boulders line the water's edge.

Feeling relaxed near Shui Hau

Pandanus fruit

Shek Lam Chau

Leopard crawling through a gap in the rock

Colourful rocks along the coast

At one time I climb out and Cathy stays in the water. I can see just how effective the current is at moving her ahead of me. I climb back into the water, squeezing between the narrow space of a huge boulder cracked in two.

We take a break, sitting on the rocks, mesmerized by the gentle swell of aquamarine water rising and falling rhythmically on the boulders. The distant islands line the horizon.

We arrive at a little beach, bright orange pandanus fruits ripen on the tree. The beach is edged by an ochre-yellow cliff. Further on we leopard crawl through a hole in the rocks which are patterned in red and pink stone. A small cove comes into view revealing a dark sea cave surrounded by turquoise water.

We walk over flat rocky shelves, jumping into the sea to swim past steep cliffs, climbing out to continue along the rocks. The water is cool and refreshing on this sultry summery day.

Weathering hematite minerals create beautiful swirling red patterns in the siltstone layers – Shau Hau peninsula

At the beach, life is different. A day moves not from hour to hour but leaps from mood to moment. We go with the currents, plan around the tides, follow the sun.

*Sandy Gingras*

# QUEEN OF THE COAST

South West Lantau Part 2
Fan Lau to Tai O
11.5 km / 7.1 miles
9 hours

The trail to Fan Lau winds along the coast with expansive views of the sea. The golden sun rises gently, turning the clouds soft apricot-pink, growing ever brighter and brighter.

The water shines and each rock seems uniquely lit by the almost unworldly glow of the soft morning light. Large boulders line the coast, so we enter the water and I slip on the algae covered rocks, banging my thigh into a solid rock covered in shells. That wasn't my most elegant water entrance, I'll get a bruise on my leg for sure.

Kau Ling Chung

Once we get in deep enough, a gentle current carries us along the coast. Tankers sail on the horizon. I turn onto my back, resting my head on my buoy, utterly relaxed. I close my eyes, the sun warms my cheek. I feel the water flooding my shoes, my backpack slightly floating off my back. Viridescent mountains covered in myriad trees and bushes of emerald and forest green, line the coast. The clouds are pure white against a brightly blue sky.

There has been some rain recently and the water is more opaque and murky than last week. We come across a sea cave, water rushes in and out with the swell. The cave looks dark and ominous and exactly like a large nose. We go in to explore. I stop to take a video and as I start recording, something brushes against my leg making me jump. Then Cathy yells, something has touched her too. Panic sets in and I shriek as something else wraps itself around my shin. Looking down we can see rubbish and plastic bags floating in the murky water. We've had enough surprises and leave the cave, laughing to dispel the adrenaline rush of fear.

Tai O comes into view, lying sleepily in the sunshine. Mangrove trees appear here and there among the rocks and then we enter the mud flats. We know all about the mud by now, so we aim straight for the trees. The sticky mud pulls at our shoes, but if we keep moving, we don't get too bogged down.

The daily rhythms of the tides rule the mangroves. Life here is challenging with the land flooded by briny water with each tidal flood and exposed to the heat of the sun as the tide ebbs. The soil is muddy, low in oxygen and unstable. But life has adapted in amazing ways to survive here and mangroves provide vital protection on the coast, stabilising the land from the surges of the sea.

The Lantau mangroves are beautiful. There are a variety of thriving mangrove plants here. Some mangrove trees reproduce by a process called vivipary. Seeds start to germinate while still on the parent tree, giving them a head start to life. When they drop, the tides carry them away to lodge in the mud and with roots already formed, they bed in quickly to start life on their own.

Trees also grow prop roots to provide stability in the shifting mud, lifting the tree on stilt-like supports. Aerial roots stick out of the mud like small antennae, improving the trees' ability to exchange oxygen and carbon dioxide.

It's so dense in the trees that we have to duck and twist to get through the branches and we come to a stream flowing into the bay. Thick mud lines the bottom and as I start to descend into the stream, I can feel myself slipping and sinking deep into the sludge, so I start to crawl, distributing my weight more evenly. And it works, we can move forward. The warm mud oozes between our fingers and slips over our knees.

The 'Nose' sea cave

Little crabs hustle into their holes as we approach. Mudskipper fish skip away, hop skipping over the mud and rocks. They are amphibious fish that live in burrows and have the amazing ability to live on land and breathe through their skin and mouth as long as they stay moist. They use their fins to move surprisingly quickly on the land, twisting and flipping through the puddles.

The crabs are splendid fiddler crabs, the males have one enlarged claw which they wave to attract a female. It's not easy to wave that big claw, females know, the better the wave, the stronger the male. Not to mention that the bigger the claw, the bigger the burrow, which makes a difference in incubation temperature for their eggs.

A sculptured horseshoe crab shell lies baking in the sun. Sandy yellow and dried out, the incredible construction of this living fossil is exquisite. There are fossil records of them that extend back for millions of years. These arthropods are not true crabs and are more closely related to spiders and scorpions. The Chinese horseshoe crab is an endangered species. They moult as they grow into adults leaving an empty shell on the sand.

Mudskipper – Shuttles hoppfish

Splendid fiddler crab

Red clawed crab

Horseshoe crab shell

Mangrove flower – Avicennia marina

Mangrove propagules – Aegiceras corniculatum

Mangrove flower – Kandelia obovata

Arriving in Tai O, we walk through the fishing village to finish the day by going around the small Tai O island since it is so closely linked to Lantau. We walk past the Heritage Hotel, the old police station that dealt with smugglers and pirates and walk towards General's Rock, a curving stone arch leaning against the cliff that looks like a General from a certain viewpoint.

The wind has picked up and the windswept swell crashes onto the rocks. It's so hot that we enter the water and bob and dip in the restless ocean. It's too rough to exit safely, so we keep swimming until we see a small rocky beach. As we swim along, my mind is drawn to wonder about what happened in these waters in ages past.

The last big battle fought against pirates, the Battle of Ty-ho, took place in Tai O bay in 1855. British and American forces united against 1500 pirates. Five hundred pirates were killed or wounded in the battle and around one thousand were taken prisoner. Seven merchantmen ships were rescued, and a number of war junks were destroyed by fire.

My favourite pirate story around these waters is the account of the pirate called Lue-Ming-Suy-Ming. He had a flag that claimed that he was 'Chief of the Sea Squadron' and that he only stole from the rich, not the poor. The local people didn't share this Robin Hood view of him though. When he was captured, they came out in their boats, anchored in Tai O bay and had a celebration, bringing gifts to thank Lieutenant Prebble for defeating the pirates.

At a rocky beach, there is a rock formation that looks like a queen sitting on a throne, the Queen of the Coast. It's a fitting place to get back to land and finish our day along the rocks.

Sea hibiscus flower

Sea hibiscus flowers open yellow and turn red over the course of the day

Generals Rock – Tai O

# HOMEWARD

Discovery Bay to Mui Wo
6.9 km / 4.3 miles
6 hours

Starting our coasteering journey in early spring, it is now nearly summer. Every time we ventured onto the coast, there was something new to discover about this unique island. There is only one stage left to complete our circumnavigation.

Cathy's daughter, Caitlin and friend, Kersti, come to see us off. We splash happily into the water on our way to Mui Wo and make our way across small beaches punctuated by rocky outcrops.

Swimming towards a beach, we evade a jellyfish and see something moving in the sea. Looking closer, we can see it's a bristle worm. There are two of them, sinuously moving in the clear green water. They are also called fireworms, because their bristles can cause an extremely painful rash which can cause burning and numbness for weeks. The worms are reddish on top and a fleshy pink underneath, edged with thousands of bristles along their body.

The ammunition storage area is ahead of us. Large red and yellow warning buoys float in the water around the buildings, showing where the restricted area is. We swim in an arc, aiming wide and swimming around the buoys demarcating the no-go area.

Walking over a small tombolo, we pass Man Kok village, round the last headland and Mui Wo comes into sight. Sunlight outlines a bank of steel-blue clouds covering the mountain peak of Lin Fa Shan. A fresh breeze ruffles the shining silver water of the bay, sending wavelets splashing onto the shore in endless motion. Windswept clouds sweep overhead, momentarily hiding the sky in swirling billows which form and flow into ever new shapes.

My eye is caught by bright green shells hidden in the rocks. Asian green mussels grow clustered in the cracks, each mussel has concentric rings in gemlike colours of amber, brown and emerald green.

We clamber over a boulder and arrive at a little beach to find Tom and Tanya, friends who have kayaked out to meet us, waiting there to cheer us on with the biggest smiles.

Fireworm

Man Kok Village Pier

Asian green mussels

Approaching Mui Wo

We wade waist high in the water, passing Bamboo beach. There's just a short section to go, we can hear our friends and family cheering and we arrive, right back where we started, finally completing our circumnavigation of Lantau.

Caitlin hangs handcrafted medals of sea glass and shells around our necks, we are elated. We have travelled over 100km around this beautiful island, through all sorts of weather, obstacles and injuries and have discovered the wild natural beauty of this island, so full of life.

Our journey has included the story of volcanic events and of eons of river life, all told in the incredible rocks and beaches around the coast. We've delved into the tales of pirates and smugglers. We've learnt about the stories of the desperate plight of people searching for a better life and the changing life of fishing villages as they have been propelled into the modern era of development.

Lantau holds its own unique beauty and wonder. It's a coast of stories and we've read the pages of this coastal tale with each headland and bay and with every beach and rocky shore.

Finally finished our circumnavigation of Lantau Island

# INTERESTING LANTAU FACTS

Lantau is almost twice the size of Hong Kong Island.

The Southwest Lantau Marine Park is about 650 hectares and is comprised of two parts. It provides valuable protection for the Chinese pink dolphin.

Lantau has rock carvings from the Bronze Age and a stone circle probably from the Neolithic Age.

The Emperor Duanzong of Song took refuge in Mui Wo in 1277.

Over 50 bird species breed on Lantau and over 500 different bird species live in Hong Kong or visit seasonally.

250 butterflies are found in Hong Kong of which 199 have been recorded in Mui Wo.

Hong Kong has recorded 5943 different marine species in its waters.

Beautiful shells and rocks of Lantau with our Lantau coast medal

# THANK YOU

I'm incredibly grateful to my friends and family who have helped me with writing this book.

Thank you Jono for all your amazing help with editing. Thank you John, Denise and Mr Cheung for the invaluable help with identifying and learning more about the rocks on Lantau. Jenneth, thank you for proofreading and for your extremely helpful suggestions. Thank you Caroline for your help with editing and your excellent advice. Thank you to the Hong Kong Jellyfish Project for help with identifying jellyfish. Caitlin, we love our beautiful medals that you made for us. Julian, Cindy and Merrin I appreciate your support. Thank you to my wonderful parents and in-laws, Clive, Dorothy, Guy and Diana for cheering me on in this journey. Joel, Tara and Clio, your encouragement and support mean the world to me.

Mike, Caitlin and Jono - thanks for being our on-call rescue team, glad you didn't receive an SOS from us.

Made in the USA
Columbia, SC
21 November 2022